MW01068731

the
power
of
quiet

the power of quiet

An INSPIRATIONAL JOURNAL
for INTROVERTS

MIRANDA HERSEY

Castle Point Books
New York

THE POWER OF QUIET. Copyright © 2018 by St. Martin's Press. All rights reserved. Printed in the United States of America. For information, address St. Martin's Press, 175 Fifth Avenue, New York, N.Y. 10010.

www.stmartins.com
www.castlepointbooks.com

The Castle Point Books trademark is owned by
Castle Point Publications, LLC.
Castle Point books are published and distributed by St. Martin's Press.

ISBN 978-1-250-18195-4 (trade paperback)
Cover design by Katie Jennings Campbell

Images used under license from Shutterstock.com.

Our books may be purchased in bulk for promotional, educational, or business use. Please contact your local bookseller or the Macmillan Corporate and Premium Sales Department at 1-800-221-7945, extension 5442, or by e-mail at MacmillanSpecialMarkets@macmillan.com.

First Edition: June 2018

10 9 8 7 6 5 4 3 2 1

For Nathan,
my beloved, who understands

Not long ago, introversion was considered a character flaw. A pathology. Something to be fixed. While extroverted personality traits are still overtly favored in Western culture, today we recognize that the general population is split about equally: half inclined toward introversion, half inclined toward extroversion.

Introverts embrace the profound experience of being alone—and we like it. We're naturally introspective, sensitive, detail oriented, analytical, and empathetic. Generally, we aren't fans of small talk—or big parties. We feel responsible for finding or creating our own happiness. We love being at home (with our books and pets and maybe a couple of the humans we adore most). We don't need a lot of fanfare and we don't like overstimulation. And even when we love you, we'll still send your calls to voicemail.

Those who don't identify as introverts can benefit from practices that encourage intentional quiet, solitude, and clarity. Introvert or extrovert, you need time alone to reflect, understand, and solidify your relationship with the most important person in your life: You. If *you* don't like hanging out with you, who else will?

Let's get quiet, turn off the devices, and take a long, solo, meandering walk that circles back to our most authentic selves.

The Secret Garden

Some of us depend on having a peaceful
hideout where we can shut off the "inputs"
and hear our thoughts and feelings.
Sometimes this is an internal,
visualized retreat, and sometimes it's
a physical location.

What places give you inner calm?

_____

_____

What places make you feel energized?

_____

_____

What local spaces or hideouts could you
add to these lists?

_____

_____

Do you have an imagined oasis for the times
when you need a break but can't get away?
If so, describe it here:

_____

_____

_____

_____

_____

The Retiring Kind

INTROVERSION AND SHYNESS are often linked or used synonymously. As many introverts will attest, however, introversion and shyness are quite distinct—and not inherently connected. Introversion is a preference; shyness is a fear.

On a scale of 0 being not shy at all and 10 being extremely shy, where do you put yourself? Circle the number below:

0 1 2 3 4 5 6 7 8 9 10

On a scale of 0 being highly extroverted and 10 being highly introverted, with ambiverted in the middle, where do you put yourself?
Circle the number below:

0 1 2 3 4 5 6 7 8 9 10

How do your responses on these two
scales interrelate?

_____

_____

_____

_____

What is your personal definition of introversion?

_____

_____

_____

What do you like about introversion?

_____

_____

_____

_____

Beloved Beasts

ANIMALS ARE OUR STEADFAST companions in solitude. Pets allow us to be ourselves. They're good listeners, they're comfortable with silence, and they refrain from criticism. In fact, sometimes animals seem preferable to people.

What pet(s) do you have right now, if any?

_____

_____

_____

_____

Who are, or were, your most memorable pets?

_____

_____

_____

_____

In what ways do animals help you to become
more yourself?

_____

_____

_____

_____

If animals aren't your thing, what facets of the
natural world fascinate you?

_____

_____

_____

_____

Solitude is fine
but you need someone to
tell that solitude is fine.

Honoré de Balzac

Routine Stop

SOMETIMES we rely on autopilot more than we realize. If we're only as good as our worst habits, might we benefit from a routine check?

What are three things you do every day that serve you well?

1 _____

_____

_____

2 _____

_____

_____

3 _____

_____

_____

What are three things you do every day that don't serve you well?

1 _____

_____

2 _____

_____

3 _____

_____

What do you want to do to address the second three things?

1 _____

_____

2 _____

_____

3 _____

_____

If you're lonely
when you're alone,
you're in bad company.

Jean-Paul Sartre

Check the Thermometer

Pausing to reflect on your mood
can offer insight into what lifts you up
and what weighs you down.
Consider the variations in your mood today.

CIRCLE ANY OF THE WORDS below that describe how you felt today. Add your own:

energized   focused

resigned   wilted

determined   content

quiet   capable

distracted   restless

heavy   overwhelmed

joyful   _____

tired   _____

anxious   _____

What brought about those feelings?

_____

_____

_____

_____

_____

_____

_____

Friday Night Delight

Visualize your ideal Friday evening.

Who, if anyone, are you with?

_____

_____

What are you doing?

_____

_____

_____

_____

Where do you eat and what do you
have for dinner?

_____

_____

_____

_____

_____

_____

What time do you go to sleep?   _____

Is your ideal Friday night substantially different
from any other night of the week?

_____

_____

_____

_____

_____

_____

The Space Between Us

EVERYONE NEEDS a different amount of time alone. For some of us it's just a few minutes, while for others it's most the day. Consider how much time *you* need to feel rejuvenated and balanced.

How much time did you spend alone today?

Was it the right amount? Explain:

_____

_____

_____

_____

_____

I need at least _____ minutes/hours
of alone time per day.

I need at least _____ minutes/hours
of time with others per day.

What happens when you don't get enough time
alone? How is your mood affected?

_____

_____

_____

_____

_____

_____

Virtual Connections

SOCIAL MEDIA allows us to connect with people at arm's length—which is a mixed blessing. It's a love it or loathe it dynamic. We may enjoy being able to express ourselves and socialize from behind the buffer of a screen, but social platforms are inherently addictive (for both introverts and extroverts) and full of minefields, so we need to keep a close eye on how much time we allot to the dopamine-driven interwebs.

The average American adult spends about two hours on social media platforms every day. How about you? Consider keeping it real by keeping a time log. You may spend far more time on social platforms than you realize—or ultimately feel good about.

How much time I spend on social platforms daily, on average: _____

How much time I would like to spend on social platforms daily: _____

Check off the ways that will help you minimize intrusions and support your introvert self.
Add more of your own.

- ☐ Limiting how many people you follow or "like"

- ☐ Taking social media vacations (you might be surprised by how much you get out of an extended social media hiatus)

- ☐ Keeping smartphones and laptops out of the bedroom

- ☐ Adopting a "no social media before 9:00 am or after 8:00 pm" rule

- ☐ _____

  _____

- ☐ _____

  _____

To be in company,
even with the best, is soon
wearisome and dissipating.

I love to be alone.

I never found the
companion that was so
companionable as solitude.

Henry David Thoreau

Proud and Not So Loud

WESTERN CULTURE celebrates stereotypical "extroverted" traits, such as being talkative, outgoing, and enthusiastic. While introverts can also be talkative, outgoing, and enthusiastic—when we choose—we have innumerable other positive qualities.

WHAT ABOUT YOU? Inventory your favorite personality traits below. Star the qualities that reflect your introverted side.

_____   _____

_____   _____

_____   _____

_____   _____

_____   _____

Describe yourself on your "worst" days:

_____

_____

_____

_____

_____

_____

Describe yourself on your "best" days:

_____

_____

_____

_____

_____

_____

_____

Loneliness

is the poverty of self;

solitude

is the richness of self.

Mary Sarton

More than Enough

INEVITABLY, we find ourselves surrounded by other people well beyond our appetite for company. What are ways in which you might get a short solo break in the midst of other people needing things from you? Here are some ideas:

- Excuse yourself for a long bathroom break; hide away with something to read.

- Wave your phone around to indicate that something or someone requires your attention; step into another room.

- Take a drive to the grocery store for a few essentials or run an "urgent" errand.

What are some escape-to-solitude tricks
you've used in the past?

Table for One

SOME PEOPLE can't imagine going "out" alone. For others, it's perfectly natural. How do you feel about:

Eating at a restaurant alone?

_____

_____

_____

Going to a movie alone?

_____

_____

_____

Traveling alone?

_____

_____

_____

How does being alone enhance or diminish
these experiences?

_____

_____

_____

_____

Would you like to commit to
taking yourself out on a "date"
once a month? If so, start a list
of things you'd like to do:

_____

_____

_____

_____

_____

Silence
is the
mother
of truth.

Benjamin Disraeli

Pick a Number

SOMETIMES we want to delve deep into an activity by ourselves—and sometimes we like to do things with others. What's your pleasure?

Things I enjoy doing solo:

_____

_____

_____

_____

_____

Things I like doing with others:

_____

_____

_____

_____

_____

Peanut Gallery

HAS ANYONE TOLD YOU that you aren't social enough, aren't talkative enough, aren't outgoing enough? Has anyone chastised you for declining an invitation, accused you of being "antisocial," or insisted that there must be something wrong with you for not jumping at the chance to do XYZ?

If you've faced this kind of criticism,
who were the critics?

What kinds of things did they say?

_____

_____

_____

_____

_____

_____

What do you want these people to know
about you?

_____

_____

_____

_____

_____

_____

_____

Our culture made
a virtue of living
only as extroverts.
We discouraged the
inner journey,
the quest for a center.
So we lost our
center and have
to find it again

Anaïs Nin

Sit for Life

THE PRACTICE OF MEDITATION is a tremendous way to align solitude, silence, and self-care. Starting every day with a meditation practice is one of the very best things you can do for yourself.

1. Determine a place and time when you will have both solitude and relative quiet.

2. Set a timer (10 minutes to start; 40 minutes or longer for the more experienced).

3. Sit in your preferred meditation posture (if you're new to meditation, sit upright with your feet solidly on the floor and a hand on each thigh).

4. Close your eyes and take several really deep breaths, holding briefly at the top, and exhaling fully after each.

5. Allow yourself to breathe slowly and naturally.

6. Count your in-breaths, starting at 1 and going to up 10. After 10, restart counting at 1.

7. If your mind wanders and you lose track of counting, start over at number 1. No chastising.

In what ways does a meditation practice
support you as an introvert?

_____

_____

_____

_____

In maintaining a meditation practice,
regularity is your friend—and your foundation.
While early morning is often ideal, select the
best time of day for your practice and respect
that commitment to yourself.

early morning   *afternoon*

morning   *evening*

mid-day   *right before bed*

Silence

is the universal refuge,
the sequel to all dull
discourses and all
foolish acts, a balm to
our every chagrin,
as welcome after satiety as
after disappointment.

Henry David Thoreau

Breathe Easy

BREATHING DEEPLY is an excellent way to call up quiet and solitude even when you don't have them. A full, intentional breath puts you right back into your body, reconnecting you to your quieter self.

Spend some time thinking about your breath.

How often do you catch yourself barely breathing?

How often do you realize that you're driving hunched over the steering wheel, lungs compressed by bad posture (or a similar realization)?

_____

_____

_____

_____

What practices might you adopt to foster more mindful breathing?

_____

_____

_____

_____

_____

_____

True Colors

SOMETIMES introverts adopt extroverted behavior simply to fit in or make life easier. We might even enjoy doing so, on occasion. But in general, being someone you're not is exhausting. And it feels kind of like cheating—on yourself.

Think of people with whom you interact on a frequent basis. With whom do you find yourself acting in ways that aren't authentic?

_____

_____

_____

_____

_____

_____

What kinds of things do you do or say
that feel forced?

_____

_____

_____

_____

Why do you make these choices?

_____

_____

_____

In thinking about these dynamics, what changes
might you want to make going forward?

_____

_____

_____

_____

_____

Sharing Silence

INTERPERSONAL SILENCE evokes strong emotion.
A lapse in conversation is often categorized as
"awkward," or, conversely, "comfortable." Silence,
when ill-timed, can be "deafening."

When a group conversation lulls, do you try to fill
the gap, or do you let it run its course?

_____

_____

_____

_____

_____

_____

_____

With whom do you comfortably share quiet?

Who will you try to add to this list in the future?

Friendly Foliage

HOUSEPLANTS AND GARDENS foster equanimity.
Tending to the green things that depend on our
attention is a nice point of restoration.

What kinds of plants, if any, are in your care?

_____

_____

_____

_____

How do you feel about this vegetation?

_____

_____

_____

_____

_____

What, if anything, would you like to change about your houseplants or garden?

_____

_____

_____

_____

_____

_____

If money were no object, what kind of indoor plants or outdoor garden would you like to have?

_____

_____

_____

_____

_____

_____

A little
while alone
in your room
will prove
more valuable
than anything else
that could ever
be given you.

Rumi

RSVP

IT'S OK to be that person who leaves the party early (or politely declines altogether). Considering the list below, for each item:

1. Put a checkmark next to events you'd enjoy.

2. Cross out anything you'd avoid at all costs.

3. Put a question mark next to events you *might* want to attend, depending on specifics.

- ____ Coffee with a friend
- ____ Evening with friends at a bar/restaurant
- ____ Cocktail party
- ____ Dinner party at a friend's house
- ____ Big bash
- ____ Office party
- ____ Networking event
- ____ Costume party
- ____ Backyard/porch barbeque
- ____ Board-game night
- ____ Birthday party for a child
- ____ Girls'/Boys' night out

___ Baby shower

___ Bridal shower

___ Bachelor/Bachelorette party

___ Wedding

___ Funeral

___ Fundraising event

___ Game-day party

___ Holiday party

___ Open mic

___ Dance party

___ Pool party

___ Book group

___ Movie night with friends

___ Live pro or collegiate sporting event

___ Concert

___ Theatrical event

___ Direct sales party (Avon, Pampered Chef, etc.)

___ Karaoke night at a local bar/restaurant

___ Protest march

___ Religious passage event (baptism, bat/bar mitzvah, etc.)

___ Religious service

What feelings does this list evoke?

_____

_____

_____

_____

_____

What are the common threads between
the items you selected?

_____

_____

_____

What are the common threads between
the items you crossed out?

_____

_____

_____

_____

_____

Host(ess) with the Most(est)

DO YOU ENJOY ENTERTAINING friends and/or family in your home? Considering the list opposite, for each item:

1. Put a checkmark next to anything you like to host (or would like to host, if you had the room).

2. Cross out anything you would avoid hosting at all costs.

3. Put a question mark next to items you *might* want to host, depending on specifics.

_____ Coffee with a good friend

_____ Coffee with an acquaintance

_____ Brunch

_____ Cocktail party

_____ Small dinner party

_____ Large dinner party

_____ Big bash

_____ Book group

_____ Board-game night

_____ Backyard/porch barbeque

_____ Movie night with friends

_____ House concert

_____ Art party

_____ Game-day party

What feelings does this list evoke?

_____

_____

_____

_____

_____

Speak to Me

AH, THE DELIGHT of having a friend with whom the conversation never runs dry. The kind of friend who shares your interests and always has something fascinating or witty or hysterical to relate; the kind who is exactly your shade of self-effacing and appreciates your sense of humor.

Meaningful conversation, in just the right dose, is essential for most introverts. We love to dive deep with someone who is equally willing to connect in a way that feels "real."

With whom do you share a strong conversational kinship?

_____

_____

_____

How often do you spend time with these people?

_____

_____

_____

Is this the right amount for you? _____

What, if any, changes do you want to implement to facilitate more time with your favorite conversationalists?

_____

_____

_____

_____

_____

Nourishment

EMOTIONS PLAY A KEY ROLE in our relationship with food. Look closely and you'll see a strange and circuitous intersection of food, hunger, eating, solitude, loneliness, love, pleasure, vulnerability, sadness, sensuality, body issues, self-medication, and self-compassion.

Which of the elements above feel relevant to you?

_____

_____

_____

How do those elements interrelate?

_____

_____

_____

What is your experience of food in relationship to
solitude? Do you eat differently when you're alone
versus with others?

_____

_____

_____

_____

_____

If anything has come up for you in this exercise
that merits further discovery, note that here:

_____

_____

_____

_____

Singing in the Shower

WHAT DO YOU ENJOY doing only when completely alone? Do you sing? Dance? Play violin? Do stand-up routines for the cat? Chances are, there's something—or a handful of things—that you do often but only by yourself.

What are your private hobbies?

_____

_____

_____

_____

_____

_____

Why don't you do these things in front of other people?

_____

_____

_____

_____

_____

What would it take for you to perform any of these activities for others?

_____

_____

_____

_____

_____

If you are alone you belong entirely to yourself.

Leonardo da Vinci

Think Inside the Box

LET'S PUT EVERYONE you spend time with through the sorting hat. Think over the past month or two. Among all the people you interacted with—at home, at work, in your community—list the 10 people with whom you spent the most time. For these purposes, that means people you spent time with in "real" life; not those you only interacted with at a distance.

1. _____
2. _____
3. _____
4. _____
5. _____
6. _____
7. _____
8. _____
9. _____
10. _____

Use this chart to categorize the people with whom you spend the most time.

How I would describe them	My Feelings About Them		
	Positive	Neutral	Negative
Introverted			
Extroverted			
Ambivert/ Not sure			

What do you notice, having added the names to the chart? Is any box more populated than the others? Did you make any discoveries about the people with whom you spend your days?
Note your thoughts:

_____

_____

_____

_____

_____

_____

_____

_____

_____

_____

_____

_____

_____

*I want to
be with those
who know
secret things
or else alone.*

Rainer Maria Rilke

Solo Beginnings

Thinking back to childhood, consider
your earliest memories of solitude.

Where were you, and what were you doing?

_____

_____

_____

_____

_____

Did you feel good about being alone, or did you feel uneasy?

_____

_____

_____

_____

_____

_____

What beliefs about solitude did your family instill?

_____

_____

_____

_____

_____

_____

_____

*The more powerful
and original a mind,*
the more it will incline
towards the religion
of solitude.

Aldous Huxley

Pen Your Peace

WRITING AND SOLITUDE are very old friends. Whether keeping a regular journal, writing for your own enjoyment, or writing for an audience, writing is a record of focused intention—however brief the writing stint.

What kinds of writing do you enjoy?

If you keep a journal, do you need quiet and solitude for journaling? Or are you able to jump in, regardless of what's going on around you?

_____

_____

_____

_____

_____

_____

How might you foster more time for writing?

_____

_____

_____

_____

_____

_____

Sleeping Beauty

SOUND SLEEP is (ideally) a celebration of silence and, depending on your domestic situation, a revelry of solitude. Good sleep in the right quantity is a way to avoid numerous physiological issues.

Research shows that spending a few minutes each day in silent mindfulness meditation (focusing on the breath and the present moment) can improve sleep, even for those who suffer from insomnia.

What is your ideal minimum amount of sleep?

_____

What is your ideal maximum amount of sleep?

_____

What would you like to do to improve
the quality of your sleep?

_____

_____

_____

_____

_____

_____

_____

_____

_____

_____

Silent Retreat

EVEN THE QUIETEST AMONG US can go deeper into silence and its gifts. Consider attending a silent retreat, or creating one of your own. Scheduling solitude and silence reaps rewards, including heightened awareness. If you can't pack off for a week or two at a meditation center, you might be able to schedule a weekend afternoon for speech-free solitude.

Where might you be able to spend an afternoon alone and silent?

_____

_____

_____

_____

What appeals to you about spending an extended period speech-free?

_____

_____

_____

_____

What concerns you about spending an extended period speech-free?

_____

_____

_____

_____

Without
great
solitude,
no serious
work is
possible.

Pablo Picasso

Walk in the Splendor of Solitude

WALKING EPITOMIZES the beauty of solitude. We engage our senses, inhabit our bodies, and connect with the world around us on our own terms. Research shows that solitary walking can improve memory—and walking yields a treasure trove of health benefits.

Where do you like to walk?

_____

_____

_____

_____

_____

_____

How can you schedule more walking time—
solitary or otherwise?

_____

_____

_____

_____

_____

_____

_____

How do you feel about walking by yourself?

_____

_____

_____

_____

_____

_____

_____

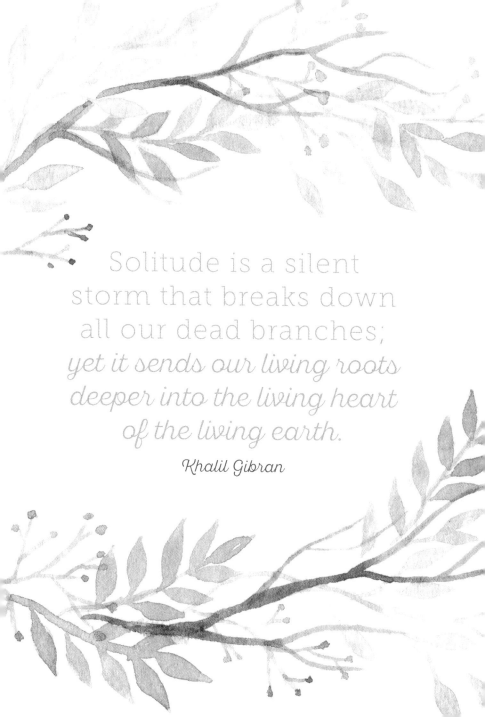

Solitude is a silent
storm that breaks down
all our dead branches;
yet it sends our living roots
deeper into the living heart
of the living earth.

Khalil Gibran

Shrink Up

OUR POSSESSIONS are part of the "noise" of our lives. Paring down to the most cherished and essential possessions helps reduce that background din so that we can focus more clearly.

How do you feel about the amount of stuff in your life?

Do you need to edit down your possessions,
or just improve household organization?

_____

_____

_____

_____

_____

_____

What is your ideal vision for what you own
and how you live?

_____

_____

_____

_____

_____

_____

_____

_____

Practice the Quiet Within

ACCESSING INTERNAL QUIET is a muscle we can work to develop. Here's an exercise for doing just that.

1. Go to a busy coffee shop by yourself.

2. Procure your favorite beverage.

3. Find a seat facing away from the wall.

4. Tune into the room; avoid listening to anything on your phone.

Detail everything you see around you. Describe the décor and the other patrons. Describe what you smell and taste. Note any snippets of conversation you overhear. Use vivid language.

_____

_____

_____

_____

_____

What other strategies have you developed for coping with noise, crowds, or chaos?

_____

_____

_____

_____

_____

_____

Reduce Your Footprint

LIVING QUIETLY is inherently connected to reducing consumption. The more we reduce, reuse, and recycle, the more we live with intention. The less we buy and obtain, the more we foster appreciation of what we already have.

Looking at your lifestyle as a whole, in what areas are you successfully conserving?

_____

_____

_____

_____

_____

In what areas do you feel like you're wasting money or resources?

How would you like to reduce consumption and acquisition?

The Music of Solitude

WHAT DOES SOLITUDE sound like to you? Is it Louis Prima playing on repeat? Verdi? Netflix on autoplay? Is your soundtrack silence? Birds in the trees? Or many different things?

What type of music do you like to listen to when you're alone?

What type of music do you like to listen to when you're feeling quiet?

_____

_____

_____

_____

_____

If you made a musical playlist to represent what you experience in solitude, what 10 songs or tracks would you include?

1. _____

2. _____

3. _____

4. _____

5. _____

6. _____

7. _____

8. _____

9. _____

10. _____

Your solitude will be a
support and a home for you,
even in the midst of very
unfamiliar circumstances,
and from it you will find
all your paths.

Rainer Maria Rilke

Home Sweet Home

INTROVERTS are unfailingly homebodies. We can't help it: We like having a cozy buffer between us and the outside world and don't want to give it up, even temporarily, if we can avoid it.

To your recollection, what is the longest stretch of time you've gone without leaving your home?

Do you ever get cabin fever? If so, what brings it on?

During daytime hours, where in your home do you spend the most time?

_____

_____

_____

_____

_____

_____

What areas of your home do you love the most?

_____

_____

_____

_____

_____

_____

Early Birds and Night Owls

IF YOU LIVE WITH OTHER PEOPLE—particularly if you have young children—quiet and solitude can be scarce. One way to claim a quiet window for yourself is to get up before everyone else does, or stay up an hour later.

Which end of the day suits you best for quiet and contemplation?

morning   or   *night*

To accommodate an early or late personal practice window, at what time do you (or would you need to) wake up? Draw this time on the clock.

What time do you
(or would you need to)
go to sleep? Draw this time
on the clock.

Great ways to spend your window of solitude:

Meditate   Note other ways here

Journal   _____

Read   _____

Exercise   _____

Plan the day   _____

What are your thoughts on developing or
strengthening an early/late window for solitude?

_____

_____

_____

_____

_____

_____

I don't hate people, I just feel better when they aren't around.

Charles Bukowski

Work It Out

RIGOROUS PHYSICAL EXERCISE draws us inward and drowns out the chatter. The internal quiet can be such a relief—even if you're not a hardcore endurance athlete.

What types of vigorous exercise do you like—or have you liked in the past?

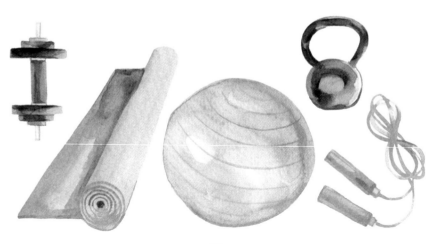

What new types of exercise would you like to try?

As an introvert, you typically feel most energized and stimulated alone or in a small group. Given that likelihood, how can you change your workout routine to better suit your personality?

Sacred Ground

SPIRITUAL PRACTICES—whether organized or independent—are predicated on quiet introspection. When we focus, quiet the mind, and connect with our larger purpose, the unnecessary noise and distractions of life fall away. And it works for theists, agnostics, and atheists alike.

Religious or spiritual practices you engage in or attend regularly:

_____

_____

_____

_____

Religious or spiritual practices you would like to engage in or attend regularly:

_____

_____

_____

_____

How does religious or spiritual practice enhance
your experience of introversion?

_____

_____

_____

_____

_____

_____

_____

Turn it Down

THE WORLD HEALTH ORGANIZATION deems noise pollution a "modern plague." We may be bombarded by stimuli in the outside world, but we can control what we allow into our homes and personal workspaces. Noise induces stress in humans, as does overstimulation. Be fastidious about every beep, buzz, flash, image, energy, symbol, vibration, and sound you invite into your home.

- Disable the automatic notifications and alerts on your phone and computer. Enforce a strict "need-to-be-notified" rule and only use it for time-sensitive events that you might otherwise forget.

- If you don't know how to remove a notification or alert, Google the problem and you'll find the solution.

Look around your home. Does what you see and hear foster quiet and calm, or discomfort and stress?

_____

_____

_____

_____

_____

_____

What can you do to be a better curator of what you allow in your home and workspace?

_____

_____

_____

_____

_____

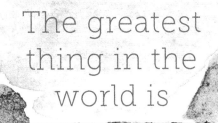

The greatest
thing in the
world is

to know how to
belong to oneself.

Michel de Montaigne

Evening Unwind

WE'RE SO BUSY GETTING THINGS DONE.
Sometimes we need permission to just be, rather
than pushing to accomplish one more thing on the
endless to-do list. If you work from home and/or
work for yourself, the boundaries between work life
and personal life can be blurry or altogether absent.

No matter how driven you are, you'll be happier,
more productive, and less distracted if you adopt an
end-of-the-work-day ritual. Whether you engage in
this ritual at the end of your paid work time or after
the kids are asleep and you really feel "done," settle
on a regular time of day for your business-is-closed
routine. This ritual will help you transition into
being, rather than doing—with a bonus investment
in the coming day.

Ritual elements to consider:

- Review the day and plan the next; update your calendar, schedule, and to-do lists. Sketch your plan for tomorrow. Note your three most important tasks so you know exactly what you're doing when you start work.

- Resolve not to check e-mail until the next work day. For most of us, e-mail is not a matter of life and death. Neither is texting, for that matter, so put your phone on do-not-disturb mode as much as possible.

- Note three things that you're grateful for in a gratitude or abundance journal.

- Tidy up your workspace so that your return in the morning feels pleasant.

- Drink a tall glass of water.

- Read one page in an inspiring book.

- Do something physical for at least one minute: jumping jacks, a yoga sequence, a plank, or run up and down a flight of stairs.

- Set your intention for the rest of the evening. How do you want to spend your time? Decide now, rather than letting fatigue and inertia lull you into an activity that doesn't serve you well.

- Have a cup of herbal tea or decaf coffee.

Map your own end-of-day ritual here:

_____

_____

_____

_____

At what time of day will you perform your
end-of-day ritual? _____

On what date are you going to implement your
new routine? _____

Deep in Thought

SILENCE REPLENISHES mental resources and empowers deep thinking. In fact, silence can literally promote brain cell growth in the hippocampus, which governs learning, memory, and emotion.

Silence also releases tension in the brain and body. Interestingly, research shows that sitting in silence for just two minutes has a more relaxing effect than listening to two minutes of "relaxing" music. When your brain has less external stimuli to process, you can access deeper, richer thoughts.

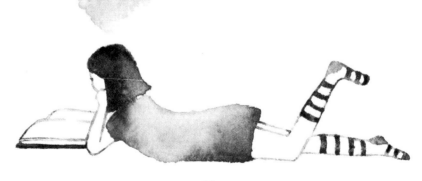

On a typical day, where might you be able
to secure a few moments of complete silence?

How might you be able to weave short periods
of silence into your life?

Think back on your "smartest" accomplishments.
How was silence a factor in your successes?

Bodywork

EMBODIMENT is an excellent way to get quiet, centered, and focused on the present moment. One way to get grounded in your physical self is by doing a body scan. Here's how.

1. Sit comfortably and breathe naturally. If you're alone, you can close your eyes—but you can also do this practice with your eyes open, surrounded by other people, and they won't notice.

2. Starting with your toes and moving upward toward the feet and then ankles, focus on each of your body parts in turn.

3. When you find tightness (rigidity or contraction), consciously release that tension. Try to "breathe into" the area of tension.

4. From toes to crown, the process can take a few moments or half an hour, depending on how much time and attention you want to invest.

What areas of tension did your body scan reveal?

_____

_____

_____

Was it difficult to relax fully? _____

What did you notice about this experience?

_____

_____

_____

What day-to-day situations might serve as cues to
remind you to silently and methodically scan your
body for tension, even when among other people
(such as making a cup of tea or sitting down at the
start of a meeting)?

_____

_____

_____

_____

Natural Wonders

WE MAY NOT KNOW for sure about the sound of a tree falling in a forest with no one around to hear it, but we do know how much introverts appreciate— and thrive on—being in nature. In addition to a ream of physiological benefits, connecting with the outdoors is a powerful conduit for connecting with yourself.

What is your experience of being alone in nature?

_____

_____

_____

_____

What do you like to do alone in nature as an adult?

_____

_____

_____

_____

If you aren't able to spend as much time in nature as you'd like, how might you schedule more of the great outdoors?

_____

_____

_____

_____

_____

_____

Domestic Bliss

MANY DOMESTIC TASKS are excellent ways to revel in a bit of solitude and quiet (vacuuming notwithstanding). It might look like you're just hard at work—but, turns out, you like doing the dishes because the simple, methodical process is an opportunity to just be yourself, immersed in the task at hand.

Opportunities for domestic solitude:

- Washing dishes
- Loading and unloading the dishwasher
- Folding laundry
- Dusting
- Sweeping
- Vacuuming
- Washing floors
- Making the bed
- Decluttering
- _____
- _____
- _____

Which of your household tasks might serve as small pockets of quiet and/or solitude?

_____

_____

_____

_____

_____

_____

_____

_____

_____

_____

_____

The soul
that sees
beauty may
sometimes
walk alone.

Johann Wolfgang von Goethe

Creative Superpowers

CREATIVITY brings a wealth of physiological benefits. While ambient noise supports creative flow for some, sensory distractions in their many forms can impede focused immersion. Solitude and quiet, which foster focus and productivity, are also the bedfellows of creativity.

What do you consider to be your ideal environment for creative work?

_____

_____

_____

_____

_____

_____

_____

_____

What creative work do you like
to produce in solitude?

_____

_____

_____

_____

_____

_____

What creative work do you like to produce
in collaboration with others?

_____

_____

_____

_____

_____

_____

_____

Take a Solo Trip

TRAVELING ALONE isn't only for the unattached loners among us. Taking a trip by yourself can be a transformative experience. At the very least, you don't have to negotiate where to go for dinner or what to do the next day. You can make new friends if you feel like it, or just enjoy your own company while you take in a new place.

What is your experience with solo travel?

_____

_____

_____

Where would you like to visit, all on your own? When might you be able to make these travel plans?

_____

_____

_____

_____

_____

Space Around the Edges

(not knowing)

In Buddhism, "not knowing" is the practice of accepting—and embracing—that we don't always know the answer. Embracing "not knowing" allows you to let go of the preconceived ideas that limit you from truly seeing.

The next time you're a passenger in a car or out for a walk, allow your gaze to move from object to object on the horizon.

The elapsed time between your eyes landing on an object and your ability to give it a label may only be a few nanoseconds. Purely *seeing*. Not thinking, not analyzing. Not knowing. In time, through practice and awareness, you can linger in that sliver of openness.

After you've practiced this exercise, note your
observations here:

_____

_____

How might you practice "not knowing" throughout
the course of your day?

_____

_____

Are there areas in which you might be able to
slow down in making decisions, judgments,
definitions, or analyses?

_____

_____

Two's Company

WHILE INTROVERTS are often mistakenly labeled antisocial, introverts know better. We like engaging with people we enjoy, under the right conditions (we just don't *need* the company of others in order to recharge). Spending one-on-one time with people we care about can remind us of who we are—in ways that solitude cannot.

Who are your favorite people to spend time with, one-on-one?

In what ways do these relationships enrich your life?

_____

_____

_____

_____

How do you most enjoy spending time with these favorites?

_____

_____

_____

_____

Do you generally feel replenished or depleted by these interactions?

_____

_____

_____

_____

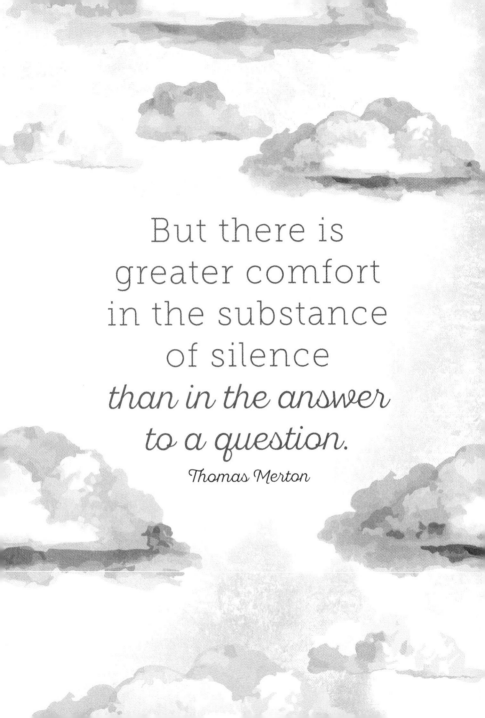

But there is
greater comfort
in the substance
of silence
*than in the answer
to a question.*

Thomas Merton

Daydreamer

BEING ALONE enables you to be completely yourself. This state of authenticity is excellent catalyst for daydreaming, recalling memories, or mind-wandering. Called "self-generated cognition," these processes can improve your ability to perform complicated mental tasks, increase intelligence, promote relaxation, and boost memory.

Were you an active daydreamer as a child?

_____

_____

What kinds of things do you daydream about now?

_____

_____

Under what conditions do you typically find your mind wandering?

_____

_____

_____

Staying in Touch

NOT SO VERY LONG AGO, our usual means of connecting with friends and family were the telephone and the United States Postal Service. Today, we have a wealth of ways to stay in touch with people we care about.

How do you prefer to communicate? Make checkmarks in the rows at right indicating how you prefer to connect with friends and loved ones at various removes.

	People you live with	People in your vicinity	Connecting long distance
Face to face			
Telephone			
Text			
E-mail			
Video chat			
Handwritten cards/letters			
Social platforms			
Other:			

What does this chart indicate about your communication preferences?

Literary Love

AS A SELF-IDENTIFIED INTROVERT who is at this moment holding a book, you probably already know that reading and solitude go together like chips and salsa.

The beauty of reading, of course, is its ability pull you out of any location or situation and transport you elsewhere. Through the power of a book, you can sink deep into solitude while packed onto a crowded, rush-hour bus. So, while it's delightful to read while luxuriating in actual solitude, reading can provide an experience of solitude while within the throng.

Ways to access more solitude through reading:

- Trade evening screen time for the pages of a book.

- Visit your local library, that font of peace and quiet.

- Listen to audiobooks on your commute.

Where do you most enjoy reading?

_____

_____

_____

_____

How would you like to increase your reading time
in the near term?

_____

_____

_____

_____

Introversion Insight

IMAGINE you're going to deliver the commencement address to a group of graduating college seniors. This isn't an ordinary matriculation, however; every member of the graduating class is an introvert. Reflecting on your experience and understanding of introversion, draft a short "How to live well" speech to guide these young introverts as they embark on the next phase of their lives. What advice and inspiration do you have to offer? What can you say about navigating the benefits and challenges of introversion? What feels important to impart?

"On this auspicious day...

For it is in your power to retire into yourself whenever you choose.

Marcus Aurelius